Down the Road

By E.K. Baer

Down the Road

First Edition, 2018

ISBN 978-1718696983

Indie Published by E.K. Baer

www.ekbaer.com

Dedication

—

To babi and děda

&

As always, to Mom and Dad

Also by E.K. Baer:

A Collection of Poems

Contents

———

Down the Road

When I Open my Eyes to the Morning

———

I open my eyes,
Let the ghastly light in,
And breathe in the lustrous air
As I savor the fresh
Fragrances of the sun.
My mind mourns the dusk of my dream
As my feet automatically
Slip out from under
The cozy blanket,
And settle on the cold morning floor.
My arms extend
To pull open the blinds.
I shudder
As the bitter light penetrates my skin
And rolls down my spine.
The hair on my neck stiffens
So I listen to my body's message:
I duck back into my bed,
Laying prostrate against
The warm mattress.
I turn away from the window
To let the sun soothe me
Back to sleep.

I Look to the Window

———

On the bed of time I rest peacefully

As I awaken languidly yawning

I look to the dark window a few feet

Away for some comfort of sunlight but

Find none.

I try restlessly to find sleep, but can

See no more than an unmade bed where it

Used to lie.

I drowsily slip out of my blanket

And look to the window, but find no sun.

Nothing even alluding to the morning.

So, I pick up my coat and walk outside

Barefoot.

I feel the tickling grass, but no frail dew,

Nor do I see any hint of light low

In the chalkboard of a sky. Will there be

Morning? I wonder in my own placid

Incredulousness.

I retreat back to my room in despair.

Gloomily I sit on the windowsill

Staring at my feet, calling on my friend,

The Sun

The steadfast, splendid rise of something new,

I grasp a book and curl up in my bed

Cold now.

I turn on my lamp, hoping to read

But the written words rudely fade before

They reach my mind. I look to the window,

Thinking maybe my lamp juxtaposes

The Sun, hoping that this night of dread has

Come to an end. But no, the night is still

King.

Placing the book on my nightstand, I bite

My chapped lip. What will I do now?

I try again for sleep, but sleep is still

Missing.

Am I tired? My mind is numb. I look

To the dim window, one last hopeful time,

Thinking surely the Sun will have arrived

By now.

But no. I am mistaken. The slothful

Sun has not yet come to be the bell of

The day.

My giddy thoughts collide. Well, I surely

Can forgive the Sun for being late,

And yet —

How could the Sun ever do this to me?

I sit up as I look to the window

Hoping the sunlight will finally reach

My eyes…

Five Thirty

The clock strikes five thirty,
And like a bell, dusk rings,
Its echo tangible to the eyes.
The Sun sets fire to the crisp bark
Of the tired auburn fall trees,
Making them burn a vivid orange.
Five thirty, you bring the dusk,
The fall of the orange Sun,
And the rise of the mirroring Moon.
This beginning of the end
Is my favorite time to transcend
As the day sheds its rays of light and
Puts on its starry-night gown.
The Sun sets its alarm clock
Each day for this symbiotic time
When its tiresome shift ends.
Five thirty,
The fall of the shining pumpkin
The rise of the silver medallion.

Born in the Night

———

Horror only strikes
At nightfall, when it cannot
Be seen advancing.

And when it attacks,
It all changes when the light
Shines through the windows.

Some people move on,
And go back to their old selves.
Those are but a few.

Those who cannot cope,
Will spend life chasing demons...
And most people will.

Frozen

———

Cold ambitions,
Dreams that can only come true,
When stepping on the back of another.
Hearts frozen solid,
Thinking only of themselves,
Silently plotting
Domination.
Tricking others into false friendships,
Creating plans with ulterior motives.
Nothing will stop them
From getting what they want.
Nothing at all.
They blindly trample over people's feelings
And will settle for nothing less than
Domination and respect
That, however, come only
Out of fear.
They shove everyone into
An eternal winter of Feelings
With their hearts frozen solid.

The Fight

———

They greet coldly by
Flaunting their piercing teeth.
They circle each other
As a sensation
Builds between their glances.
They pounce, kicking up the snow,
Revealing the mushy soil.
Who will win?
For one will win.

Pain

He is GONE.
He IS gone… forever.
Never to come back.
He is gone.

The harsh, cold pain of loss
Paralyzes me
And makes it barely possible
to move, to eat, to breath.

I run, run from the pain,
Leaving those who turned me
Away when I tried to tell them
Of my loss and sorrow.

Tears clot in my eyes,
And I realize, I
I cannot run away,
Away from the pain.

But I will run forward,
Taking it all with me.
I must live a life, for
That is what he would want.

I must find the people,
Who will not reject me.
People who will hold my hand,
Wipe away my tears
And help show me the way.

For Danny

History's Abode

———

Deep in history's inexorable abode
Rest the victims of a tragedy,
The tragedy of the unsinkable ship
The RMS Titanic
That sank, dragging with it hundreds
Of lives.
We now slowly discover
The treasures of those lost.
And within those treasures,
The secrets of lives once
Lived.
Lives once
Exposed to the fresh sea air.
Those lives are described to us
Within the leather walls
Of the bags that the now placid hands
Once carefully packed and touched.
Journals lie inside the bags,
And within the journal
Secrets were once written.
Even what resides inside history's abode
Can be discovered with the turn of a handle
And the push of the door,

And all that now resides

Deep inside

History's abode

Will once more live in the sun.

The Lumberjack

———

With prodigious force,
The callused young lumberjack
Hauled the newly chopped wood back
Into the back of his company's dirty,
Old, toughened truck
And as soon as he arrived
His unsteady frozen legs
Gave way under him and he
Quickly fell down to the cold
Earth that was spread out like a carpet
Below his numb feet. Not one
Concerned glance was cast in his
Direction, and even his own
Workmates were way too busy
Thinking about themselves to
Think about the cold, trembling
Lumberjack whose job was much
More taxing than their own.
The young man who shivered so
Fragilely was left to his
Own fate by those he had thought
Were his friends. There was only
One man good enough to cross the divide

And lift his comrade from the unrepentant,
Icy ground. This man held out
His dirty hand to lift the Lumberjack
Back up into the frosty sun.

Turning Ground

———

I sit here inaudibly,
Watching a withered petal
Fall to the abrasive ground.
Your willowy breath cuts through
The tingling, bashful, cool air
And my breath gets put on hold.
Turning ground is what you do
Furtively enough to make
Your murmur wail like thunder.
Incising a crack between
The land that joined us as friends.
You turn away from my cries
And my want to keep our bond.
Without so much as a glance
Back at what you left behind.
You grasp my enemy's hands
While so precipitously
An apocalypse of dusk
Enshrines my crushed heart
As you nonchalantly freeze
My desolate trembling soul.
How hard can I try to stop
You from turning ground on me?

How blue to know that you will
Turn ground on my foe soon, too.
I close my eyes and dream that
The bold and olden petal
Has since sprung roots that fill up
The isolating abyss
Of the harsh and hostile ground
I stop dead in my tracks of
Loneliness and give way to
Gallant confidence.

Live Louder

In the muted Hall of Silence
A resilient voice broke out.
"Must we all spend our precious
Minutes in silence?"
The voice cried out for attention.

No eyes turned.
No ears listened.
No mouths opened.

"Come on, live louder!"
The voice urged.
"Come on everyone!"
But still, everything
Remained the same.

"Those who are silent are cowards,"
The voice preached.
"And those who are silent in
This Hall of Silence are the most cowardly!

Live louder!"
The core of humanity trembled,
Stirring a reaction within the silenced
Minds surrounding the voice.
Everything stopped.
Fear.
Worry.
Terror.
The oppressive silence was no longer ruler of the land.

And then, gallantly,
Like sunlight blazing through a window,
Voices began to illuminate the room.
They chanted,
"LIVE LOUDER! LIVE LOUDER!
LIVE LOUDER! LIVE LOUDER!"
Until the very core of the Earth heard
Them chanting.
And if the core of the Earth had a mouth,
It would have chanted with them.

Turn Up the Radio

———

I turn up the radio
And let the music pulse in my
Ears for a minute.
The lights are dark,
And the Sun is gone.
I feel the echo of the music throughout
Me.
I feel the placidness that one feels when
Alone.

Yet, I am not alone.

Through the darkness, a breath rings loudly.
The music softens into thin air.
"Turn up the radio," I say,
But receive no answer.
"Turn up the radio," I repeat.
Nothing.

"I said turn up the radio!" I yell,
And the music picks up
Where it left off.
"Finally…" I murmur calmly.

But then
Sweat starts dripping down
My forehead.
"Who's there?" I call, but
Receive no answer.
"WHO'S THERE?!" I scream.
The lights flash on—

And I see my right hand
On the radio dial,
And my left hand
On the light switch.

It is… me.

Noise

———

I had the single most peculiar moment last night.
It seemed, within the time constraints of the moment,
As if all the noises around me were merely originating
Inside my head.

When I straightened myself and settled,
Quietly listening for the sounds that usually
Ring about me,
There was a deathly pallid silence which
Took a gloomy toll on my spirits
In the moonlight.

The noises I had heard previously seemed to
Be suddenly much more dull and doleful
Until at last they disappeared into
A diminuendo of time.

I was then enveloped by the shattering clamor
Of sleep coming upon me.
This sensational sound was so vivid
That the rest of the world

Disappeared, becoming a memory lost in time.

As life drifted from reality into a dream,

The depth of alacrity of the world began to

Turn

Itself towards the morning.

And then…

Diminuendo

———

It died off,

Leaving a sliver,

A splinter

Of sound in my ears.

Sugar Coating

———

There are individuals everywhere,
Trying to pretend that they are helpers,
Good people.
On the outside they smile
And say:
"I will volunteer!"
But on the inside, they say:
"Who cares?"
They put a thick layer of sugar coating
On everything,
Thinking that no one can see through it.
But, as this poem did come to be,
It is made manifest to me,
That the sugar coating
Is as transparent as glass.
Is it normal to smile so big
That your cheeks stretch?
Is it normal to laugh
And talk so high-pitched
That you sound like a mouse?
Cheesy.

That's the word.

Cheesy.

A perfect description for

The behavior of the sugar coaters.

And if you put cheese and sugar together?

Yuck!

Unknowledgeable Knowledgeables

———

All the little people in the world,

With their little bit of power,

Strut around while using it.

Some use their power to help others,

While others use it to usurp.

Some of those people make

You smile and laugh.

And the others make

You frown and shake your head.

All the little

Unknowledgeable knowledgeables

Are everywhere.

But the rest of us

Knowledgeable (un)knowledgeables

Have to stick together

And make a barrier against

The things that make us frown.

Decision

———

t-r-ap, t-r-ap.

Patience.

Patience.

Have patience where all else

Would walk away.

Remain.

Remain.

Remain after

the rest of the world has fled.

t-r-ap, t-r-ap.

Think.

Think.

Think quickly – your fate

is in your hands.

Do.

Do.

Do what you feel is right –

you are your own master now.

t-r-ap, t-r-ap.

Is.

Is.

Is it right for you to sit here,

t-r-apping your fingers on the table?

No.

No.

No, it is not right –

you are a fool.

t-r-ap, t-r-ap.

Coward.

Coward.

You will become a coward

if you flee.

But.

But.

But will you be

A rightful coward?

t-r-ap, t-r-ap.

Fool.

Fool.

You would be a fool

to stay.

Yes.

Yes.

Yes, you would be a fool

if you left now.

Will.

Will.

Will you be

a fool or a rightful coward?

t-r-ap, t-r-ap.

Leave.

Leave.

Leave – your

life is at stake.

Dream.

Dream.

What if this is just

a dream?

t-r-ap, t-r-ap.

Don't.

Don't.

Don't be a fool,

Don't be a coward.

Be bold and walk

to the beat of your own drum.

t-a-p, t-a-p, t-a-p!

Third Place in the 12 and under category of the Ventura's Art Tales Contest

Long Way Down the Road

———

The fog thickens round me, blurring my tracks,

Making the road ahead nothing more than darkness.

Through the darkness, you follow my footprints,

Though they are hazy.

When I weep despairingly, sitting at a fork,

Not knowing which path to take,

You take my hand and wipe my tears to the ground,

And a map grows, showing me the way.

A long way down the road,

The sun will clear the fog,

And all that are just dreams now, will be reality then.

In a world of decisions, bends, and turns

You guide me to make my own path,

A new one,

That might one day be followed by many others.

So, I trek through the brush, and conquer all my fears.

Feeling loved and loving, two things we own,

At the core of our hearts.

You supply more than enough love for one,

Even more than enough for an army.

You are a savior when I am ready to give up,

A savior of my future, a savior of my future's history.
You sing me to sleep when trouble comes tumble-weeding down
the path.
It is a long way down the road to go
But I know you will be there to guide me through it.

When I get lost, you will find me,
And guide me back to my path,
Even though the fog is thick, and my footprints blurred.
I can march confidently down the road, and not have a concern.
It is a long way down the road,
But you will guide me.
You follow me through forests and deserts,
Mountains and oceans,
Anywhere the path leads me, you are there,
Teaching me as I go.
The low meadow to the high meadow,
The east plain to the west plain.
You follow me.
It is a long way down the road,
And I am willing to walk it,
As long as you are with me,
To guide me and to teach me and show me where to go
When I am lost.

Without you I would give up,

Quit.

Fail.

But you always convince me that

Even though the road is long,

I will make it to the end, and that

Even though it seems endless,

One day I will look back and be glad

That I went down that path.

But that is a long way down the road.

Through it All

———

Through sadness you always make me smile,
Through blindness you help me see,
Through deafness you show me how to hear,
You are always there for me, no matter what happens.
Your love is always there, no lock to pick to see it.
It is always a knight in shining armor
When the walls do not hold.
You are always there for me,
Through it all.

A Letter to a Friend

———

My Dear Friend,

Please allow me to call you that,

For I have no words to express

How very dear you are to me.

You support me through every bend

In the road I am taking in life.

Your hand is never blind,

And when I sob, it wraps around my hand.

Your love and protection are genuine,

And true.

There are no words to show how much support

You give me. You lend me your smiles,

So that I can wear them and be infected

By your joy. You bring me a sweater to hug

Me

When I need an embrace.

Or chocolates to sprinkle the day with sweetness.

You know me better than anyone else,

Including me.

Thank you for being you

And for always being there for me.

Our Love

———

If skies are blue, our love is tranquil —
Two people carving hearts in bark in the sun.
If thunder rolls and roils in the sky,
Our love is a gallant haven from the blustery rain.
When spring's flowers blossom,
Releasing their fragrances into the air,
Our love is sweet, like rose petals
Dotted with crystal raindrops
On the cool, dew-covered grass.
When autumn leaves descend,
Our love is gilded,
Shining like the harvest sunset.
In summertime, our love is innocent,
Like lavender swaying in the breeze.
In wintertime, our love is warm —
A fire that toasts us from head to toe.
From the year's dawning till the dusk of time,
Our love will continue to shape our hearts.

Milk and Cookies

———

I would jump off a twenty-foot cliff,
Into a rushing, rippling river
If you held my hand and jumped with me.
It would be our daring endeavor

I think we may just be a perfect match,
Just Like Milk and Cookies.

If you came with me, right by my side
I would leave my small town and home land,
And travel across the wide oceans,
To live a life that we would make grand.

D'you think we are made for one another,
Just like Milk and Cookies?

I will give you my fragile, warm heart,
If you promise you will not break it.
You must protect it, and be gentle,
And show me your heart is the best fit.

We are wonderful and perfect as one,
Just like Milk and Cookies.

I will run through the streets of Paris,
In search of an alcove, to keep dry…
As water gushes from the fiery sky,
If you are there with me, my oh my.

We are truly meant for one another,
Just like Milk and Cookies.

Lyrics of an original song for the film "Next to Love"

The Two of You

A new chapter in the book of bonds, another endless string that links you. One more tie that cannot be split, no matter how far away you are from one another. You share roses, chocolates, secrets, memories and each other. These are merely six of the thousands, millions of things that make you one. Tomorrow, just one more page, one more bridge. Forever, gazillions of stories to tell. But it does not end at forever. Forever is too near, too close to right now. There will always be a connection, between me, and both of you. Just between you. A link that will keep spelling 'we', beyond infinity.

For my parent's anniversary

The big, long branch of the climbing tree

———

The big, long branch of the climbing tree,

Extends an arm out to the children

Running across the valley around him.

The big, long branch of the climbing tree,

Has the most brilliant memories

Of all the times when laughs were

Sprinkled upon every corner of the meadow

Below it and around it.

The big, long branch of the climbing tree

Is a refuge to all

That own glorious

Imagination.

The Optimist

———

The optimist stood proudly
On the Earth's mighty podium and called out,
"The world can be hate-free! It can be! It can be!"
People passed by, shaking their heads, saying,
"No, no, it cannot be. There will always be a hater."

But the optimist persisted: "Then lend them a smile!
The world can be hate-free! It can be! It can be!"
The people exchanged sad smiles.

But the optimist persisted.
Nothing could bring her down.
She was not afraid to be called stubborn
Because she knew the truth:
The world COULD be hate-free!

But the optimist also knew
That she would not be taken seriously
Unless someone else joined her cause.

And one day, sure enough, somebody did.
The smallest of somebodies joined,
And that someone was a child
Who truly believed
That the world could be hate-free.

Together they stood proudly on the Earth's mighty podium
And together they called out,
"The world can be hate-free! It can be! It can be!"

People passed by, shaking their heads,
But their ears listened
And their hearts opened,
Even just a little,
And they became a tiny bit optimistic themselves.

And in that moment,
The world did become a better place,
Just like the optimist had predicted.

Winner of the 12 and under World Without Hate Art + Writing Contest 2018

Reflection

Diamond dewdrops of water
Roll down the twisted stems of
Copious, seeded green ferns
And gracefully distort my
Fondness for the gallant moon
In the scenic, clear water.
The most unstinted mirror
That belongs to the marriage
Of day and night,
The knightly Moon and the dyaus Sun.

Than Ever Before

———

The grass was greener than I had ever seen before.

The Mountains were oh so stormy, dark, and cloudy.

Grey-blue streams trickled down the hills into little creeks.

It was magic. There could be no other explanation.

Colors of the Rainbow

———

The hills were green, oh so green.

Little blue streams trickled down from icy peaks.

Purple flowers, as bright as the sun,

However wee they may appear, they sure caught my eye.

The golden-haired sun shone over the ripe strawberries,

Coloring them an even brighter hue.

The electric blue sky, home to the sun and fleecy white clouds,

Warmly embraced the emerald hills.

Deep in a verdant valley, surrounded by grassy hills

Lined with blue streams rushing all around,

And dotted with flamboyant purple flowers,

The sun smiled bright yellow from the cobalt blue sky

As an affectionate rainbow

E x t e n d e d

Across the valley and over the hills.

The Mist

———

The icebox of the morning
Chilling the gallant, crystal
Air that roams wildly around.
It rouses shyly over
The timid River, slyly
Greying the tamed atmosphere
Shielding us from the angered
Sun.

Winner of the Ventura County Writers 2018 Poetry Contest 12 and under

43

The Reflections

———

An immersed reflection,
A mimic of reality,
A dream of what may exist
Draws rings by the muddy bank.
A tired Weeping Cherry Tree
Attentively inches toward
The crystalline water.
She rejoices at seeing
Her baby petals playfully distort
Her almost tangible image
On the moon-sprinkled surface.
Stars light-heartedly dabble at
the fresh, raw reflection
that calls the water home.

Autumn

———

The welcoming bouquet of a freshly baked apple pie
Piquantly soaks the sun-drenched air.
People of all ages crave to play all-day
In all the charismatic piles of crunchy leaves.
The sidewalks are lined with lush auburn trees,
Languorous branches slowly waving hello.
A few red-crested woodpeckers sound off a lively rhythm
As they chip away at the swinging trees.
Chirpy children flounce around,
Slipping out of their nifty book bags,
Dashing into prodigious piles of ginger leaves.
Sweethearts unfurl soft summoning blankets
Over the verdant dew-shielded grass,
And picnic under the shade of the olden oak trees.
The whooshing winds whisper mysterious stories
Into vivacious ardent ears.
Autumn is the time of sentimental syrupy love!

The Call of the Birds

———

Each morning the call of the birds
Gently wakes me
Into the ghastly light of morning.
I roll off my blanket,
Slip out of bed.
I walk to the window pane,
And watch all the birds bustling about.
I feel free and airy as I watch them,
And I have a reverie that one,
Just one,
Will come tap on my window.
I will open it up,
To let the bird fly to my hand
And perch on my outstretched finger.

The birds singing to the sun
Each morning
Are a reverie.
Mothers teach their
Youngsters how to fly.
The first fragrance of Spring
Blossoms about the wind.
Birds dot the shrubs by the shallow creek,

Some dipping down to take a sip, or a bath.
I open the window to fully
Experience the gilded magic,
But even that is not enough.

I tip-toe downstairs,
Shove my feet into slippers,
And my arms into a jacket.
I run outside
And as I climb up one of the trees.
I scare the birds away,
But after only a minute
They all come back.
I recline in the tree
As the birds sing around me.

Purple Moon

———

The Moon's purple rays were twinkling down onto the pond.
Dancing water lilies incrusted its grassy moist bank.
It had just rained, only moments ago
And drops of water dripped down from the edge
Of the curved, green leaves.

The water rippled as the frogs erratically sprung
Between the round, floating lily pods.
In the purple tinted water, the Moon's reflection
Rested for the night.
A soft wind blew, pushing the lily pods under
A branch of an over-hanging fern.

Boing, boing, a bunny bounced to take a sip of
The cool, luscious shimmering water.
A startling giggle cut through, and the bunny scampered away,
Too afraid to find out who the laugh belonged to.
And then with a few thumps, four human feet rested
By the side of the pond
Two were large and two were small.

The mom and her daughter looked up and watched how
The sheep dotted the nearby hills like dandelion seeds,
Up, and up, and up they went…
Grazing on the fresh grass as they roamed.
The sheep must have thought it was the day,
Since usually they would be sleeping the night away.
Kept up tonight by the Moon oh so full shining brighter than ever,
Over the memories, life and magic of the pond.

Second Place Winner in the 2017 Write On! Poetry Contest

I, the River

———

I start out as a small trickle mischievously
Scrambling over pebbles, barely catching
A glimpse of the youthful, silly Sun.
I am blasé and growing.
I flourish and spill into a bustling city
Where citizens venerate me,
Build bridges to decorate me,
And people from far and near
Keep me company.
Here my life is peaceful,
And only the wind can ruffle
My gilded surface. Hundreds
Of smiling faces peek from the
Windows of the castle:
The flamboyant jewel of my bank.
Weddings with wild, waltzing
Feet spin on my muddy borders.
Singing and laughing never cease
During these countless
Times when many are together.
My journey then comes
To an end as I spill into the ocean
Bearing strong ships.

I join numerous other waters, my friends,
Who have ventured here as well.
We rejoice at being joined again
And our stories overlap and fold to
One another.
I am summoned into the heavens for
A playdate with the Sun.
When I leave, the Sun cries, shedding her
Tears into a dried-up brook where I
Set out on my journey all over again.
I start out as a small trickle mischievously
Scrambling over pebbles…

As the Ducks Do

———

As the Dawn slowly creeps to my window,
I lay in my bed and listen to
The ducks recall their past year
And plan their new one.
They quiddle and quaddle,
Argue and disagree
Over the things we humans
Rarely stop to think about.
They contemplate a myriad of thoughts
That rarely touch our brains
Like how the world can change now and
Why it is not changing.
They talk freely about the year ahead
As they remember the yesteryear,
With all its failures and successes.

We should all do as the ducks do,
Be a community, open and free,
One big content family.

We, too, should quiddle and quaddle

About what could be,

Disagree until we agree.

Share knowledge,

Share our pond.

We should do as the ducks do.

The Waltzing Flame

——

A flame vivaciously dances in front of my eyes,
Its bright, thin strands of scorching red hair tickle my face.
I see my reflection in its untamed, growing spark
As well as my confidante's, whose hand I hold.

As welcoming as the fire may be,
It shifts from a place a warmth to a beast when let off its leash.
Spreading to every corner of a prairie, forest, or town.
But I will not let go of the leash.

My face feels warm as I watch the show in front of me.
Owls hoot all around, spectating spookily from the trees.
My companion in this enchantingly intimate moment
Smiles as I tell my grandfather's story about a dragon and a star.

I think of all the things a flame can be,
As my soul mate points out the reflection in my eyes,
And the echo of the fire's dance imprints on my dreams
As I fall sleep.

Honorable Mention in the 2017 Iron Horse Poetry Contest

LXXXVIII

—

Eighty-eight stories, links and bonds
To all the ancient worlds, to our
Sage ancestors and their beliefs.
An amazing plethora of
Eternal bridges plotted out
Boldly on the mute sky each night.
The stars are spectacles into
Distant worlds filled with wonders;
They remind us of our heroes
And mighty audacious creatures.
They Create a picturesque scene,
With actors waiting in the wings.
Their gaudy globular Director,
The kind old silver-haired master,
Spaces and choreographs them
In the glorious scorching show
That we observe when the night comes
Rolling around.

A Candle of Flowers

———

Embedded in a chrysalis of wax,
Petals tangibly embrace and overlap
Creating a scented masterpiece
Bathed in laughter
On a languid summer day.
When the candle softens,
The most delightful fragrance
Melts right into the air.

Jade Earrings

———

Shimmering in the dazzling sunlight,
Glowing in the darkest hours of the night,
Brightening the rainy, foggy day,
Is a pair of jade earrings.

Though I am tempted to wear them,
I know there is a time for beauty.
But as I sit in bed and watch them,
I grow weary of waiting.

I listen to their humble cadence,
As they drum against the wall mount in the wind
Gathering from an open window.
Tum, tum tum, Trum, trum trum
As it gently repeats this cadence over and over…

I snatch them and wear them,
As I want to fall asleep in their magic.
But when I touch them their magic goes away,
And suddenly I realize, that I saw no imagination in them,
Just the need for the credited name of beauty.

Evergreen Heart

———

There is a heart in the Evergreen Tree

A way down the road.

But this heart is not ordinary –

It is a true artist's heart.

It has love written

In an invisible ink within

Its rounded silhouette.

An artist is just an artist,

As a tree is just a tree,

And as a

Heart is just a heart.

But when you mix

Them together, the result is a truly

Wonderful body

Of emotional magnificence.

And then, when you add love,

It creates a grand

And desired life force – true, true love.

Beautiful Aroma

———

A thin gust of wind
Carries the smell of freshly baked
Pastries from the bakery down the road.
The scent teases my nose,
Making me stop in front of the bakery door.
I look inside and see the baker organizing
Croissants on a platter.
This beautiful aroma,
Tempting me to walk in.
This beautiful aroma,
Better than the finest of perfumes.
I cannot resist,
And so I walk inside.
"Ah! Good morning!" the baker calls.
"Good morning!" I smile. "One croissant, please."
I pull out my wallet.
"Here you go! Have a wonderful day."
The baker hands me a croissant
And leaves for the kitchen.
The beautiful aroma
Of freshly baked cookies
Tickles my nose.

A Mini Collection

———

I

The ship sails on an ocean of a million
Carefully drawn loops of blue.
The artist steps back and looks
At her masterpiece.
And within the boundaries of imagination,
The ship sails away,
Into a fresher river of gratitude.

II

Loop after loop,
Line after line,
The beauty of the artist's
Masterpiece
Seeps through the skin
And into the soul.

III

Noses nuzzling, fins flapping,
Within the heart of seaweed.
Happiness shines into the eyes of the lovers
Through the glass of the frame…

IV

Once, a likeness was drawn of a fish
Who, instead of scales, had the most boisterous
Flowers. Its eyes were grey and somber,
And its fins were dotted with weary spots,
But, the flowers along its back
Were vividly and radiantly depicted
By the artist's brush.

Pip

———

You are strong,

Little Pip.

Nose of yours not high,

Mighty Pip.

Your smile is too weak,

And your walk too childish—

That's what they say.

But you, Pip, are small yet potent.

You face the world every morning,

And you smile at everybody.

Don't let 'em tell you who to be,

Cause you are Pip.

You are made to be Pip,

And no matter how much you want

To be someone else,

You are meant to be you.

Pip.

And you should be proud,

Because you are unique and wonderful

Just the way you are.

Golden Goliath

What if Goliath were made of gold?
Would David still have fought him,
Or would David have bowed down?
Would David have been jealous,
And killed Goliath anyway?
What if Goliath were made of gold?
Would he still be a beast?
Or would he be a king?
What if Goliath were the ruler of the world?
Would David have been Goliath's servant,
Or would he have fought Goliath still?
What if Goliath were a beautiful queen?
Would David have killed Goliath then?
Or would he have kissed Goliath's hand?
What if Goliath were a God?
Would David have been so witty?
Or would David have fallen to his knees?
What if Goliath were made of gold?
Would David have retreated?
Or would he have stayed?

The Hat Keeper

———

In a cottage, down at the bank
Of the rolling, rippling river
The Hat Keeper organizes woven
Hats on sturdy walnut tables.
His door is always propped open,
And the warm smell of leather and apples
Wafts through the open door,
And lures in a passing nose.
A wall supports a shiny mirror,
Between two of the carved tables
For all the fascinated customers
Who tiptoe in and admire a hat or two.
In the corner, by a fireplace,
The old man sits and weaves hats,
To later be displayed on a wooden table,
Viewed, tried on, admired and sold.
He sits alone, gently humming a tune,
As he weaves love into his hats,
Giving them the might and the magic
To transform, inspire and empower us.

How I Met the Blue Girl

———

At last we meet, Blue Girl.
My visit is much overdue.
Your home, now Iceland – how is it?
Do you miss your birth town, Blue Girl?

Lying there in your glass case,
Vivid light shining on you…
How does it feel, Blue Girl?
Everybody bustling around to meet you.

"There she is! There she is!"
I exclaim at first sight of you.
I have been reading about you for years, Blue Girl,
And at last, we meet in person!

A soft tingling joy
Runs through my body
As I look at you, blued teeth and all.
Oh, Blue Girl, you will live on.

The Woman in Blue was a Viking who lived between 900 and 920. When she was 5-10 years-old, she moved to Iceland. Her name comes from the blue apron that she wore.

The Characters of Dawn

—

The unburnt sky blue,

Lightened by the white.

The characters of dawn

Settling in the air.

Thousands here,

Here are thousands more!

If we could only look into the sun,

We would see them all.

And look,

Here are millions more!

Her

———

Piles of silk brush the ground,

As the unruly grass climbs up the creases

Of the star dusted fabric.

Soft curls tickle her bare shoulders.

The wind spins around her,

Piercing her eyes

With memories.

Nature,

Being an artist,

Draws hoops around her conscience.

Goddess of the Wind

———

A goddess of the wind
Glides over the hilltop,
Her dogs, haltered to crisp leashes,
Glide side by side with her.
The sighing wind forms fluttery ribbons
Out of her long locks of hair.
The hounds of white lead their queen
Across the countryside,
Leaving civilization in the mist.
On the horizon, rural fantasies
Rest, waiting for her majestic arrival.

Moonward

———

The sea gently folds all its tides and sways

Moonward.

The stars glisten in the mirror of his crest,

Pointed

Moonward.

All the characters in the sky hover in position

And look Moonward,

Toward the cold-bred air

And wispy breeze.

Up into the face of the Moon.

Who are You

___

Who are you?
A frosty breath that tosses me around
And down into the unending abyss
Of unanswered curiosity?
Who are you?
Why do you not answer me?
Who are you?
Why do you step on my fingers,
Crunching my delicate bones
As I try to climb out of the abyss?
Who are you?
Why do you cut the rope, grab my ankles,
Seep through my skin and give me chills?
Who are you,
Abysmal, exquisite curiosity?

A Clamor, not Clamorous

———

A clamor, not clamorous,
A beauty, not beautiful,
An abyss, not deep,
A path with no trail…
A bluebird with no blue,
And no bird.
A plane with no wings,
And no flight.
Rain, falling up.
An invisible that is visible.
An echo that is single,
Bouncing through your ears,
Telling you the secrets
Of those you cannot hear.

Pantomimes

She falls back,

He catches her.

She screams,

He runs.

Pantomimes,

Pantomimes.

Dramas,

Dramas.

Practiced hundreds

Of times over

With various actors.

Like life.

Striking Hot

I watch the wind whistle
Through the leaves,
I hear the branches wave.
I feel the wind
Strike hot an urge in me
To do
What I usually would not.
If I could…
I would
Fly through the door
Free as the wind
With only fun in my thoughts.
I could let everything go!
I would
Charge into the fragrant embrace
Of the openhearted meadow,
And roll down its carpeted hill
All the way to the valley below.
I would not
Worry about how I look,
Or care about a thing in the world.
It would not matter to me –
Not the littlest bit.

But I would

Catch butterflies on my nose,

And twirl in the sun,

If only,

Oh, if only I could!

I would

Jump up and down,

And climb every tree.

And run with the wind,

Whistle and holler.

I would

Chase the birds all around,

Until they tell me how to fly.

The sky would strike hot

The urge to touch the clouds,

And I would

jump so high,

That I would be one with the birds.

Human hindrances aside.

Life would be

Whatever I want it to be.

No rules to break,

No walls to stop me.

I would be invincible!

I would

Weave headbands

Out of wild flowers,

And bracelets out of grass.

I would be

A fairy running wild

From dawn till dusk,

And everything in between.

I would

Run to the creek,

And glide through the water,

Jump over the rounded pebbles.

I would

Swim with the fish,

See all their treasures

And hiding places.

I would

Fly out of the water,

and shake out my hair

Like the bears do.

I would

Chase wild ducks across

The bank of the river,

And gallop in the grass,

Sun in my hair,

Butterfly on my nose,

Not caring about what the world thinks,

Human hindrances aside,

Without a wall to stop me.

Courage

———

Courage is a strike of determination and pride,
A bolt of strength that sparks a powerful urge,
A feeling that intertwines
A group of people.

Courage is the ability to wake up each morning
And show the world your character.
Courage is the ability to love,
To care,
To…

Courage is being vulnerable
And stepping out of your
Comfort zone and into
The unknown.

Courage is showing everyone
What you truly
Believe in.

Acknowledgements

―――

Mom and Dad: I would not be writing poetry without your love and support.

Ms. Dallas Woodburn: This book would not be what it is if it were not for you. I so appreciate all the ways you help me.

Babi and děda: You make every day better and you somehow make the ocean between us disappear.

Dr. Newman: Thank you for always encouraging me to be who I am.

&

To all my family, friends, mentors, and teachers who have guided me down the road – thank you.

About the Author

———

E.K. has been writing poetry ever since she was very young. She published her first book, A Collection of Poems, when she was 10 years old. Besides writing, E.K. loves science, math, and history! She also plays the violin, piano, and she sings. Traveling the world is one of her favorite things to do. E.K. enjoys spending as much time as possible with her dog Coco.

www.ekbaer.com

Made in the USA
Columbia, SC
14 February 2020